Oh, Chickadee!

BY
Jennifer Richard Jacobson

ILLUSTRATED BY
Jamie Hogan

MCSEA BOOKS

In a hole,
in a tree,
(known as a cavity)

there is a nest.

Moss and bark,
rabbit fur and
bulrush fluff
cradle the eggs.

Each one laid on its very own day.

Mama chickadee rolls the eggs.
A featherless patch on her belly
keeps the chicks warm

until...

naked chicks pip
with the help of an egg tooth—
a bony tool that tops each beak
and will soon fall off.

Mama carries the eggshells far away.
No predators
will find her clutch!

Papa chickadee brings food.
Caterpillars dangle over gaping mouths
rimmed with yellow,
so he can find them in the dark.
Squawk! Feed me! Feed me me!

Mama chickadee hisses like a snake
to protect her nestlings from danger.

Papa teases fledglings,
I have food!

But he won't bring it to the nest.
Not today.
Today is the day for being brave.
Today is the day for flying...

And for landing.

But,

it's hard
to stop,
to hold,
to balance.
Whoops!

Chickadee hops on the ground.
But not for long!

The family flies away from the nest,
yet remains together
while Chickadee learns
to find berries,
watch out for weasels,
and stay in her territory.

Then, when
Chickadee is ready,
she says goodbye to
her brothers and sisters

and goes in search of a new flock for fall and winter.

New friends forage
by hovering,
probing,
hawking,
and hanging upside down.

Sit, sit, sit, Chickadee calls
to say she's near.
Sit, sit, sit, they call back.
We're here too.

Some morsels are carried away to be eaten,
others are hidden— each one in a different spot.
Later, Chickadee will remember where
each tasty bite is stashed.
She'll eat the best bites first.

But days grow cooler,
colder, frigid.

Winds blow.
Snow falls.
New downy feathers
puff out like a winter coat
to keep Chickadee warm.

Perched on icy branches,
bird feet get cold.
Up one goes,
into fluffed-up feathers.
Now time to warm the other.

At night
Chickadee sleeps alone
in a tiny hole.
The cold
lowers her body temperature,
but shivering allows her to stay alive.

She needs so much food!
Probe, flutter, probe, flutter.
Oh, look!

Insect eggs beneath bark,

sunflower seeds on a feeder,

cones on a tree.

Someone is calling.
Is it safe?

Brave little bird
eats to keep warm.

A friend becomes a mate,
(*Fee-beeyee! Hey Sweetie!*)
carving out new holes.

*How about
this one?*
asks the
soon-to-be
father.

No, this one! dances
the soon-to-be mother.
She's the boss.
She chooses.

As days grow longer,
Chickadee grows quieter.
Secret work begins.

    While her mate searches for

    caterpillars...

She carries off woodchips.
    Shhhh!
She travels to find moss.
    Shhhh!
And rabbit fur.
    Shhh!
Quietly, she builds.

In a hole
in a tree,

there is a nest.

Until one day...

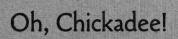

Oh, Chickadee!

GLOSSARY

Pip: break through an eggshell

Egg tooth: a sharp, horn-like growth on the tip of a beak. Newborn chicks use it to crack the eggshell. The egg tooth will disappear within the first five days.

Fledgling: a young bird with new feathers and ready to fly

Clutch: a nest of eggs or a brood of chicks

Hawking: when a bird leaves a perch and captures an insect in the air

Incubate: to keep at the right temperature so the chicks can develop

CHICKADEE CHIRPS

Here are some fun facts to share:

* This book is about black-capped chickadees. There are seven species of chickadees in North America: black-capped chickadee, mountain chickadee, Carolina chickadee, boreal chickadee, Mexican chickadee, gray-headed chickadee, and chestnut-backed chickadee.

* Black-capped chickadees weigh about four pennies.

* The familiar "chick-a-dee-dee-dee" call can mean many things. Sometimes it means "I've found food" or "Where are you? Let's come together." A long string of "dees" at the end signals danger.

* By shivering, chickadees can raise their body temperature to 100 degrees Fahrenheit, even when the temperature outdoors is only zero degrees.

* A female chickadee tends to lose the down feathers on her belly in the summer so she can incubate the eggs. She does not start incubating until the last egg is laid—that way all the eggs hatch at roughly the same time.

HOW TO GET A CHICKADEE
TO FEED FROM YOUR HAND
(It's best to try when the weather is cold, and food is harder to find.)

1. Begin by attracting chickadees to your yard. Hang a bird feeder with seeds (you can find lots of ways to make your own online). Chickadees are very fond of black oil sunflower seeds.

2. Try to fill your feeder around the same time every day. Hang around the feeder for a little longer than usual so the chickadees get used to you and know you're not a threat.

3. Keep the feeder empty one day. (Or empty the seed out.) Stand close to the feeder with seed in your hand. Keep your hand as flat and as still as possible. Be very patient.

4. Eventually, a brave chickadee will land on your hand. Try not to make sudden moves or sounds.

5. If this doesn't work, you can try this trick. Place your mitten on top of the feeder. Put seed on your mitten. Let the chickadees land on the mitten for a few days. Then empty the feeder and put the mitten with the seeds on your hand.

LEARN MORE!

Angus, Laurie Ellen. *Paddle Perch Climb: Bird Feet are Neat*. Nevada County, CA: Dawn Publications, 2018.

Davies, Jacqueline. *The Boy Who Drew Birds: A Story of John James Audubon*. Boston, MA: HMH Books for Young Readers, 2004.

McClure, Wendy. *A Garden to Save Birds*. Chicago, IL: Albert Whitman Books, 2021

Wolfson, Elissa Ruth and Barker, Margaret A. *Audubon Birding Adventures for Kids: Activities and Ideas for Watching, Feeding, and Housing Our Feathered Friends*. Beverly, MA: Cool Springs Press, 2020

*To Harlow Jones Jacobson who at this writing loves
all living things except hoppers.* — J. J.

*To Patty Wainwright, my sweet neighbor
who shares her bird wisdom.* — J.H.

Text © 2023 Jennifer Richard Jacobson
Illustrations © 2023 Jamie Hogan
All rights reserved.

Published in the United States of America by McSea Books, 2023
Manufactured by Regent Publishing Services Ltd. Printed in Shenzhen, China

McSea Books
Lincoln, Maine
www.mcseabooks.com

Cataloguing- in-Publication Data has been applied for and may be obtained from the Library of Congress.

Book design by Jill Weber / frajilfarms.com

The illustrations were drawn with chalk pastel on sanded paper.

ISBN: 9781954277151
Library of Congress Control Number: 2022919912

JENNIFER JACOBSON has loved chickadees since she fed them from her hand as a child. She is the author of many award-winning books for children and young adults. Her novel, *Small as an Elephant*, about a boy who was abandoned in a campground in Acadia National Park, won a Parent's Choice Gold award and is now in its 19th printing.   jenniferjacobson.com

JAMIE HOGAN is an illustrator of many books for children with nature themes, as well as the author of *Skywatcher*. She enjoyed learning about chickadees for this book and watching these busy birds from her backyard feeder, but they won't sit still!   jamiehogan.com